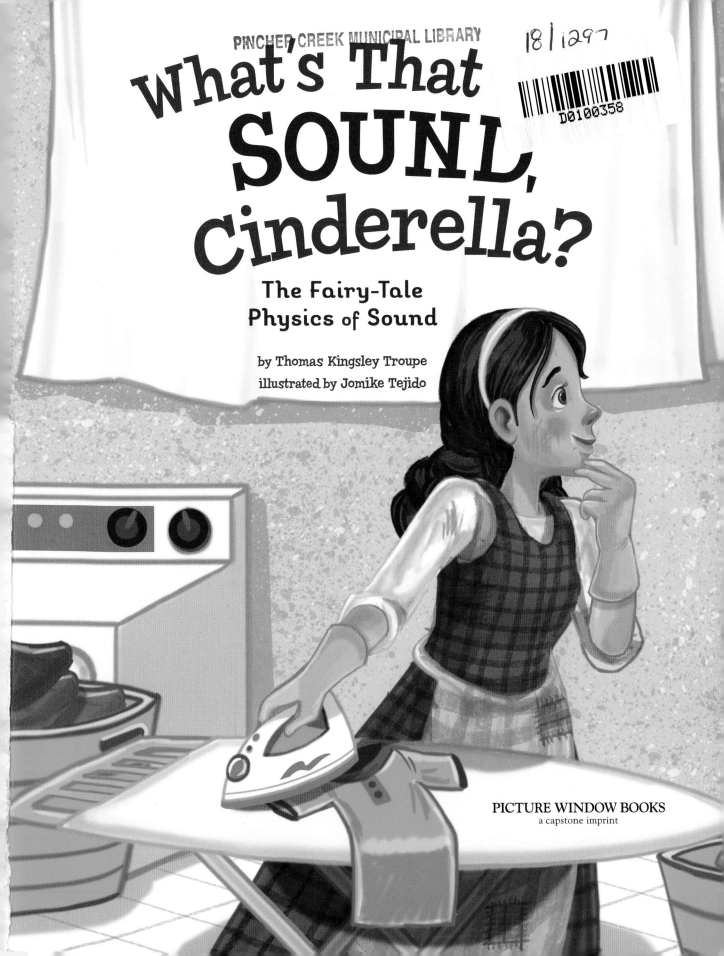

What's That SOUND, Cinderella?

The Fairy-Tale Physics of Sound

by Thomas Kingsley Troupe

illustrated by Jomike Tejido

PICTURE WINDOW BOOKS
a capstone imprint

Some time ago, in a faraway land, lived a girl named Cinderella. Sadly, her mom died, and her dad married a lady who wasn't nice. Even worse, the lady had two terrible daughters. And they were super bossy.

Day and night, all Cinderella heard was the sound of her stepsisters yelling: "Cinderella, sweep the floors! Cinderella, clean the cat box! Cinderella, unclog the toilet!"

"Please call me Cindy," Cinderella begged.

"Nope," her stepsisters said.

Every day Cindy listened to her stepsisters bark orders. She heard them sing their awful songs.

"Oh, Broomy," Cindy said to her broom. "I can hear my stepsisters' voices upstairs through the floor! The sound waves are making the kitchen ceiling vibrate!"

Broomy said nothing.

As Cindy mopped the bathroom, she heard her stepsisters'
loud dance music. *BOOM! BOOM! BOOM!* The water in her bucket
vibrated with every drumbeat.

"Goodness, I can even *see* how loud the music is," Cindy cried.

In need of fresh air, Cindy went outside. Soon she heard a vehicle approach. It was a party van, blasting its horn. The horn sounded faster and faster as the van got closer to the mansion.

Cindy watched the driver park the van and run to the front door. He rang the bell, and the sound of chimes bounced through the halls, creating an echo. Cindy's stepsisters flung open the door.

"Special delivery!" the driver said. "The prince has invited you all to a ball tonight. There will be dancing, food, and good times. Please wear your finest clothes!"

After his delivery, the driver hopped back in the van and drove away. The blasting horn sounded slower and slower as the van got farther away from the mansion.

Cindy ran inside. Her stepsisters were excited to go to the ball. She was too.

"No, Cinderella," Stepsister 1 said. "*You're* not going."

"No one wants to see *you* there," Stepsister 2 said. "You look like you crawled out of a dumpster!"

The sisters hurried upstairs and demanded that Cindy help them get ready. And she did. She curled their hair. She zipped and buttoned their dresses. The stepsisters just talked and laughed, laughed and talked.

Such noise! Cindy thought. *If only someone could hook up their big mouths to a generator. The energy from their nonstop talk could power a small city!*

Soon the stepsisters left for the party. Cindy stayed to clean up the mess they'd left behind.

"I'm sick of being treated like dirt, Broomy," Cindy said, looking at her broom.

"Then let's get you to the ball," a woman's voice said.

"Broomy!" Cindy said. "You can talk!"

"No, dear," a woman in the doorway said. "Brooms can't talk." Her musical voice made the mirrors vibrate. Her clothes sparkled. So did her teeth.

"Who are *you*?" Cindy asked.

"I'm your fairy godmother," Godmother replied. "So, do you want to go to the dance or not?"

"Yes, please," Cindy said.

"Good," Godmother said. "Then I'll need some things, dear: a few mice, a pumpkin, and a dog. Meet me out front."

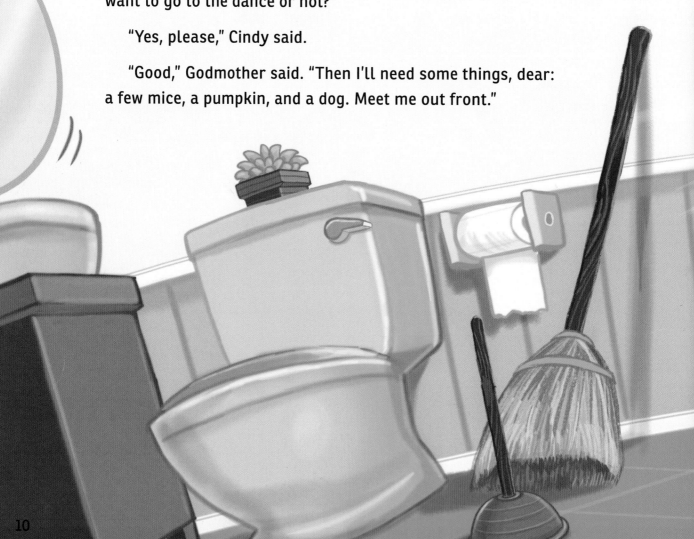

Cindy did her best to find what her fairy godmother wanted. She came back with three cockroaches, a pineapple, and Broomy.

"This was all I could find," Cindy said.

"Close enough," Godmother said. And with a wave of her wand, the three cockroaches became a team of bodyguards. The pineapple turned into a monster truck. Broomy became the driver.

"Whoa! Cool!" Cindy shouted. "But won't I need a dress? I mean, I can't wear these rags to the ball."

"Done!" Godmother said.

POOF! Cindy found herself in a beautiful dress . . . and a pair of glass high-top sneakers.

"Well, these are weird," Cindy said, pointing at her shoes.

"You're all set," Godmother said. "But know this: My magic won't last forever. The giant clock chimes at midnight. Once the twelfth bell sounds, everything returns to its original form."

"But how will I hear the clock?" Cindy asked. "I'll be inside at the ball."

Godmother touched Cindy's cheek. "My dear, sound waves can travel through all sorts of materials," she said. "They can move through air and water—even walls! They might sound quieter or louder going through different materials. You know that already. How many times have you heard your stepsisters yelling and singing when they were in another room?"

"More than I can count," Cindy said.

"Right," Godmother said. "Sound waves vibrate the molecules in matter. That vibration is what you hear with your ear. I could talk about the physics of sound all day, but you have to get to the ball! Now, go!"

Cindy hopped into the truck and was off. The truck growled like a T-rex. *RAWRRRR! RAWRRRR!*

"Wow, this truck is really loud!" Cindy shouted, covering her ears.

"It sure is!" Broomy said. "Did you know that sound is measured in decibels? The higher the decibel number, the louder the sound is. I learned that from your fairy godmother."

"How many decibels does this truck make?" Cindy asked.

"About 100 or so," Broomy answered. "Levels this high are really not good for your hearing!"

"What?" Cindy shouted.

Broomy smiled. "Exactly!" he said.

Cindy had a blast at the ball. She met important people and ate fancy food. Everyone thought she was an amazing dancer. She told the best jokes too.

"Who is that?" Stepsister 1 asked, pointing at Cindy.

"I have no idea," Stepsister 2 said.

Cindy smiled. Even her stepsisters didn't recognize her. The prince asked her to dance, and she did.

"You're a great dancer," the prince said.

"Hey, thanks," Cindy said. "You're pretty good too."

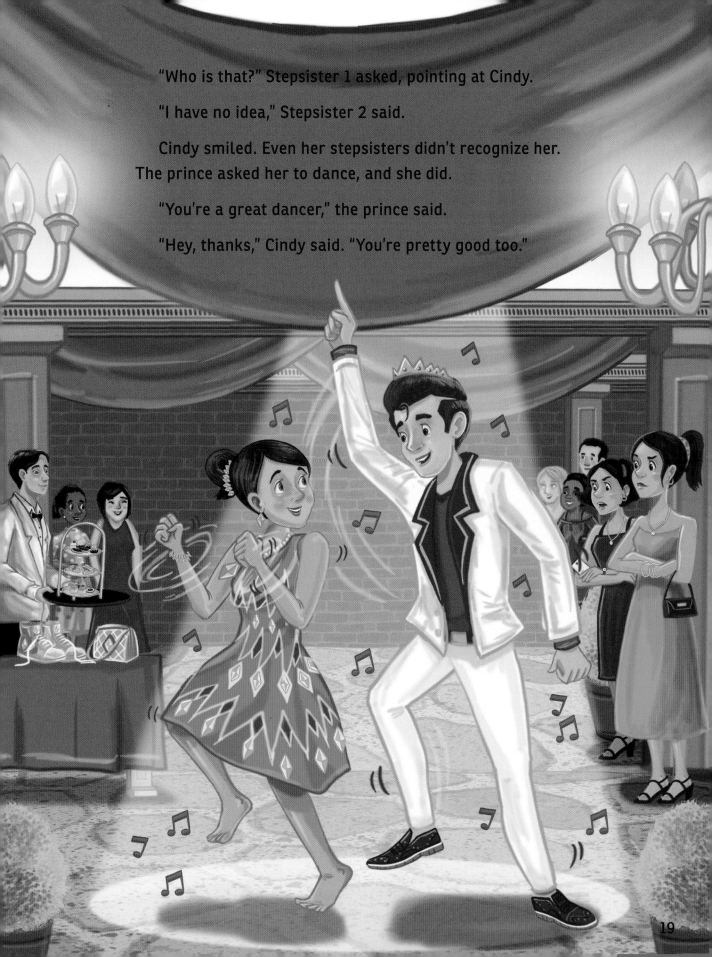

The two danced and danced, until . . . *GONG!* The giant clock started to chime. Midnight!

Sound waves traveled from the clock tower across the street and through the castle walls. Cindy's outer ear caught the sound. Her eardrum vibrated.

The vibrations then moved to three tiny bones, which pushed the sound to her inner ear. There the vibrations entered a small, curled tube and turned into electrical signals. Almost instantly, the signals zoomed to Cindy's brain and told her what she'd just heard.

"The bell!" Cindy cried. "I hear the bell! Time to go!"

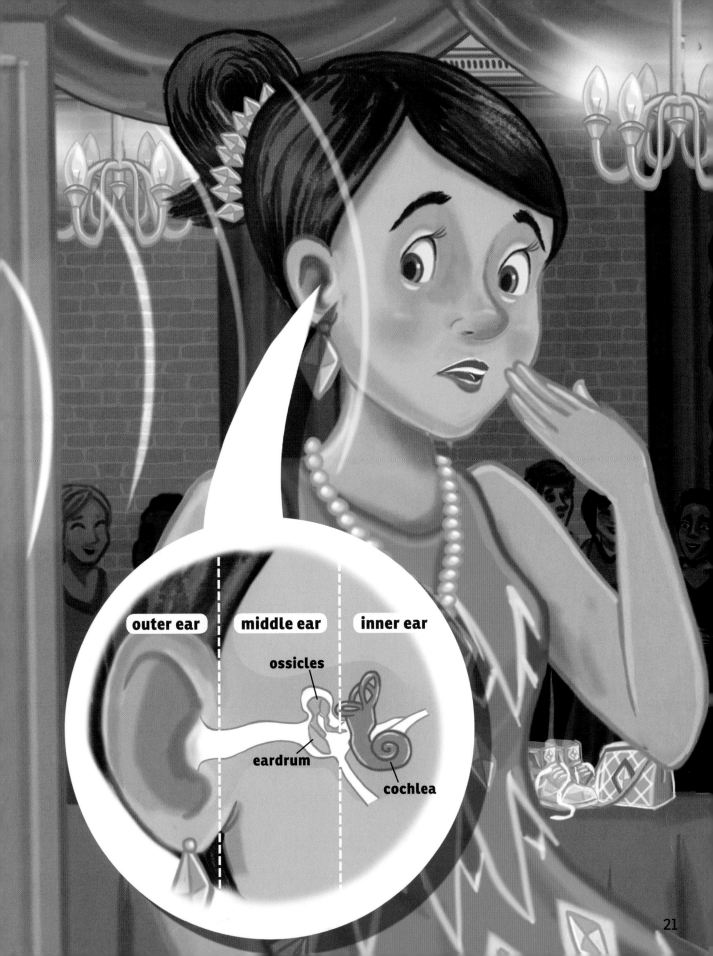

outer ear

middle ear

inner ear

ossicles

eardrum

cochlea

GONG! GONG! GONG!

The prince watched as Cindy quickly grabbed her things.

GONG! GONG!

"Where are you going?" the prince asked.

"I have to get home," Cindy cried. "It's late!"

GONG!

The stepsisters couldn't believe anyone would leave the prince alone on the dance floor. Who was the mystery girl with the amazing dance moves and sharp fashion sense?

GONG!

"Wait, I don't even know your name!" the prince shouted.

"No time!" Cindy said.

Everyone in the ballroom watched as Cindy ran out the door.

GONG! GONG!

She hopped in the monster truck, and it roared down the street. All that was left behind was one glass high-top sneaker.

GONG! GONG!

Cindy ran out of time. The monster truck turned back into a pineapple. Her driver became a broom again. The bodyguards were cockroaches once more. Even Cindy's beautiful clothes were turned back into rags.

When she finally got home, her rotten stepsisters were already there.

"You missed a *great* time, Cinderella," Stepsister 1 said, flipping her hair.

"*Such* a great time," Stepsister 2 said. "But I bet you had more fun, playing with your pineapple and broom! Ha!"

"Oh, I had fun," Cindy said to herself.

The next morning, everyone on the news was talking about the ball—and the mystery woman.

"She was the coolest," Stepsister 1 said, her eyes glued to the TV.

"Oh, and those dance moves!" Stepsister 2 said.

Cindy smiled. She watched as a camera crew followed the prince to different homes in town. He carried a glass high-top sneaker in his hand.

"My shoe," Cindy said, too quietly for her stepsisters to hear.

"He's having every girl in town try on that shoe," Stepsister 1 said.

"If it fits, she must be it," Stepsister 2 said.

A short time later . . . *KNOCK! KNOCK! KNOCK!* It was the prince, followed by a news crew.

"Good afternoon, ladies," the prince said. "I'm looking for the woman of my dreams."

The stepsisters squealed and grabbed the shoe from the prince's hand. Each of them tried to put it on. It was much too small.

Cindy quietly dusted the piano. By accident, she bumped one of the piano keys. The musical note echoed throughout the mansion.

"What about you?" the prince asked, pointing at Cindy.

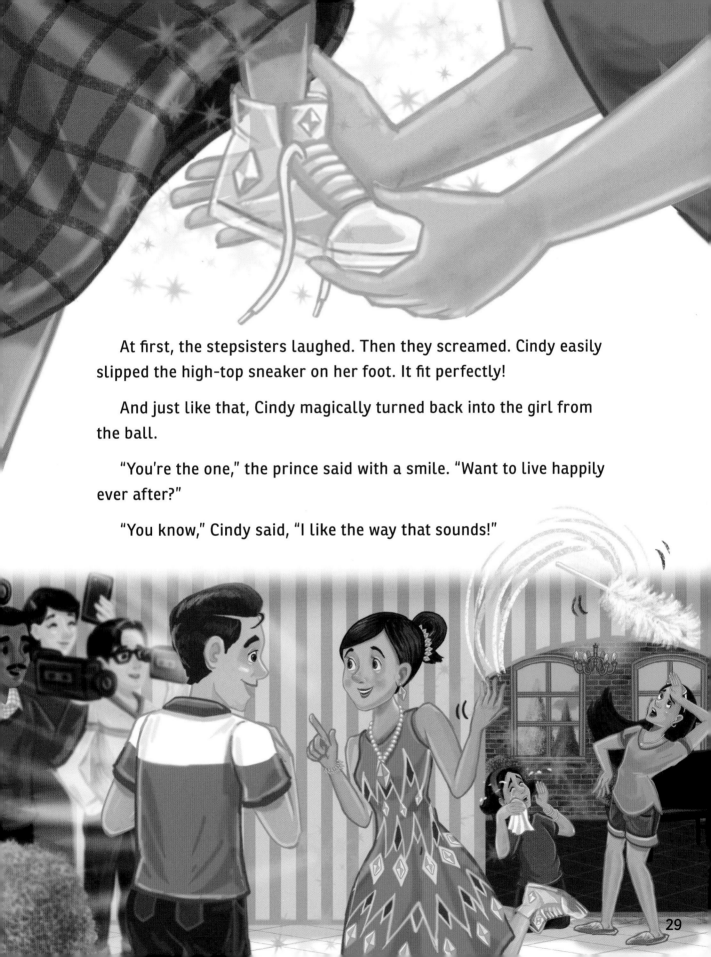

At first, the stepsisters laughed. Then they screamed. Cindy easily slipped the high-top sneaker on her foot. It fit perfectly!

And just like that, Cindy magically turned back into the girl from the ball.

"You're the one," the prince said with a smile. "Want to live happily ever after?"

"You know," Cindy said, "I like the way that sounds!"

Glossary

decibel—a unit for measuring how loud a sound is

echo—the sound that returns after sound waves hit an object

generator—a machine used to change energy into electricity

matter—anything that has mass and takes up space

molecule—the atoms making up the smallest unit of a substance; H_2O is a molecule of water

physics—the science that deals with matter and energy; physics includes the study of light, heat, sound, electricity, motion, and force

vehicle—something used to carry people or things from place to place

vibrate—to move back and forth quickly

Critical Thinking Questions

1. Use the illustration on page 21 to explain how humans hear sound.

2. Sounds over 85 decibels are generally harmful to your ears. Normally, two people talking to one another measures about 60 decibels. Lawn mowers and hair dyers are about 90. Name three other things you think are louder than 90 decibels. How could you protect your ears from these things?

3. Describe how the story ending would change if Cindy couldn't hear the clock strike midnight.

Read More

Johnson, Robin. *The Science of Sound Waves.* Catch a Wave. St. Catharines, Ontario; New York: Crabtree Publishing Company, 2017.

Rompella, Natalie. *Experiments in Light and Sound with Toys and Everyday Stuff.* Fun Science. North Mankato, Minn.: Capstone Press, a Capstone imprint, 2016.

Royston, Angela. *All About Sound.* All About Science. Chicago: Heinemann Raintree, an imprint of Capstone Global Library, LLC, 2016.

Internet Sites

Use FactHound to find Internet sites related to this book.

Visit *www.facthound.com*

Just type in 9781515828976 and go.

Look for all the books in the series!

Index

Special thanks to our adviser, Darsa Donelan, Professor of Physics, Gustavus Adolphus College, Saint Peter, Minnesota, for her expertise.

Editor: Jill Kalz
Designer: Lori Bye
Premedia Specialist: Tori Abraham
The illustrations in this book were created digitally.

Picture Window Books
1710 Roe Crest Drive
North Mankato, MN 56003
www.mycapstone.com

Library of Congress Cataloging-in-Publication data is available on the Library of Congress website.
ISBN 978-1-5158-2897-6 (library binding)
ISBN 978-1-5158-2901-0 (paperback)
ISBN 978-1-5158-2905-8 (eBook PDF)
Summary: The stepsisters yell. The fairy godmother sings. The pineapple-turned-monster-truck burns rubber on its way to the ball. For Cinderella, this evening is an enchanted STEM adventure through the science of sound. For readers, it's a treat of a fractured fairy tale, complete with an ear diagram, a key-term glossary, critical thinking questions, and a sweet pair of glass high-top sneakers.

Printed and bound in the United States of America.
PA021